Releasing &

Letting Go of

Excess Baggage!

Flush Out Darkness

Flush In Spiritual Awakening

Dr. Patricia Logan-Miles

Releasing and Letting Go of Excess Baggage
Flush Out Darkness, Flush in Spiritual Awakening
Part 2 of the *Shattered But Not Destroyed* Series
Copyright © 2015 by Patricia Logan-Miles

ISBN-13: 978-1519398444
ISBN-10: 1519398441

SOV Books
Downey, California

Printed in the United States of America

All scripture references are derived from the King James
and/or the New American Standard Versions of the Bible.

Be sure to pick up a copy of

Part 1 of this series ...

Shattered But Not Destroyed

By Dr. Patricia Logan-Miles

Go to: Amazon Books Dr. Patricia Logan-Miles

Or write: drpatmiles@yahoo.com

Forward

**By Evangelist
Leon Isaac Kennedy**

Dr. Patricia Miles (Dr. Pat) shows and displays a love for the Lord's people who are hurting and broken. Dr. Pat reaches out to nurture and encourage those who have inner wounds of abuse, abandonment, rejection, discouragement and emotional hurts and pain. When I met Dr. Pat, it was with a ministry of intercessors. It became apparent that we had a similar calling from God on *Inner Healing* to those that are in bondage. Dr. Pat is also an entrepreneur and has owned several businesses. One was with battered women and children. She is one of today's too few intercessors devoting many hours daily to prayer and studying God's Word. 'Father' has also given her a keen discernment. During the many years I've known Dr. Pat, she has shown great character and integrity; something that has become a lost treasure in today's world. This book is a tremendous tool for inner healing and restoration.

Meet the Doctor

Dr. Patricia Logan-Miles is an ordained pastor, evangelist, and international minister in healing, deliverance, and is used by God in the prophetic gifts across the United States and foreign countries. Dr. Logan-Miles was the former owner of *Creative Neighbors Always Sharing* in Los Angeles for seventeen years. Dr. Logan-Miles also produced and hosted a weekly television and radio broadcast in Los Angeles that reached over 500,000 homes. She was also featured in many aspiring African-American articles. Dr. Logan-Miles currently resides in Houston, Texas, and continues to minister healing, hope, and deliverance to men and women. Join Dr. Logan-Miles on the next page for her personal testimony.

My Testimony

Before we begin, I'd like to offer a brief testimony about my life experience as an abused and battered woman. I understand what an abusive and battered relationship can do to an individual based on my own life's experience. I have been a victim of emotional, mental, and physical abuse many times in my relationships.

Releasing and Letting Go of Excess Baggage, is Part 2 of my prior book, *Shattered But Not Destroyed.*

Releasing and Letting Go shares how healing and deliverance was a painful experience in my own life, but above all things, proved to me that the pure love of Jesus Christ can give us the security, protection and confidence necessary to overcome the trauma of abuse. In fact, there is nothing too difficult or impossible for God. (Jeremiah 32:17). The Lord can still give you the desires of your heart and it's never too late!

I was healed of a broken heart after a seventeen-year marriage without hope or prospects of a sound future. I lost all my material wealth and ended up displaced. However, my personal experience in Jesus Christ turned my life around *completely* and transformed me into a positive, self-confident person!

Being a virtuous woman of God helped me to learn that God will never leave me nor forsake me. My desire is to teach others that they have a purpose and destiny that only can be fulfilled by following God. We may fall but we can get up and look up, and move forward with great expectation that the Lord can and will heal every area of our lives.

Stop looking for a man to complete you. Let him look for you! You are a royal diadem! Proverbs 18:14 declares, "The spirit of a man will sustain his infirmity, but a WOUNDED SPIRIT WHO CAN BEAR?"

I am Dr. Patricia Logan-Miles and I was the founder of several agencies ministering to battered women and children, pregnant teens, victims of domestic violence and substance abuse, in greater Los Angeles, California. My ministry was to bring healing and deliverance to hurting women, children and families.

My former husband and I were pastors of a very successful church as well as owners of other prosperous businesses. After marrying this man of God, I became dependent on him and began to worship the man rather than God; but the Lord is a jealous God. The marriage ended due to his affair with another woman in the church. He left me, closed all my bank accounts, put a restraining order on me and took all my businesses. Then I lost my home and everything I owned, which caused me to become displaced.

This book is my testimony. God delivered me from inner torment, turmoil, inner pain, a broken heart, a shattered self-esteem, depression, resentment, betrayal, abandonment, unforgiveness, trauma, adultery and bitterness. During this time God had to allow me to suffer the inner wounds, strip me and deliver me, so that I might reach the purpose, plan and destiny he had destined for my life. But first, I had to be healed of each wound. I forgave my husband, released the inner pain to God and, as I sought him, he guided and directly healed me of each inner wound.

The Lord never desires to hurt us or cause suffering upon us, but sometimes we have to go through trials and tribulations during the transformation process. As I stated earlier, I had begun to worship the man more than God, and the transformation, back into the center of God's will, was painful, and yet the most rewarding experience of my life.

My prayer is that, as you read this book, Jesus will minister to you on how to be healed and delivered of your invisible inward/invisible wounds. *Releasing and Letting Go of Excess Baggage* will teach you how to let go of the past, move forward, and deliver you from your past and the bondages that have held you for so long. You'll soon see how you can use these experiences for your good and blessings.

The Flush Index

Introduction

For many years I was in a place of holding onto the past, always looking back at what I should or could have done to create a better outcome for my life. I could not fix or change my mistakes because I didn't know how to release and let go.

Growing up I was rejected, lonely and felt no real love from my parents and siblings, except for my brother who was my best friend. I had asthma as a child and could not play like most children, I had to be home-schooled. Later, my brother was killed in a car accident at the age eighteen and I was devastated for many years.

As a young adult, I was still holding onto these inner wounds and didn't realize that I had to let them go in order to reach the plan, purpose and destiny God had designed for my life. Therefore, I kept blaming myself for my failures and hurts, and internalized all the guilt for someone else's behavior.

In fact, guilt caused me a great deal of hurt, pain and disappointment, resulting in my shattered self-esteem. During that time, I suffered with depression and despair and existed with very little hope. I didn't know God but knew *of him*, nor was I aware that I was in desperate need of a personal relationship with him. When I entered junior high school it was difficult for me to make friends because of the sheltered life I had lived. My focus was on getting good grades and school was a way of escape for me. I had no social life whatsoever, but, thankfully, I met one friend, who became my best friend throughout my school years. During my high school years I was an honor-roll student. This was a great joy for me and gave me hope. When I graduated the only family member that attended my graduation was my mother. My father had to work and couldn't attend. It was crushed that he didn't attend my graduation but it would have been a greater surprise if he had.

Throughout the years, my father was never very sensitive or attentive toward me, which caused me to have feelings of rejection, hurt and low self- esteem. As a child, I never felt loved at home because it was never spoken or shown.

As a result of the extreme insecurity I felt growing up, I became co-dependent, the prime symptom of which is, the inability to let go and release relationships, friendships and, later in life, disappointments in my ministry life, all of which held me in bondage. In fact, I was crippled by discouragement, a broken heart and low self-esteem.

Our mothers cautioned us to keep our bodies pure, but as you might have guessed, I began looking for love in all the wrong places early on, with young men who were not sensitive to my needs and feelings. But I wanted to feel something I never felt before. I wanted to be loved. I wanted to be nurtured and held in my father's arms.

I pray that as you read this book you will be released and set free of your inward/invisible wounds and no longer look in the rear-view mirror, but look instead at God has ahead for you … and it's just around the corner!

Dedication

This book is dedicated to the Lord Jesus Christ who gave me the strength and courage to release and let go of the past. I also thank him for giving me a real compassion and sensitivity for the broken-hearted, battered women and children and those without hope.

Philippians 3:12

"I don't mean to say I am perfect. I have not learned all I should even yet, but I keep working toward that day when I will finally be all that Christ saved me for, and wants me to be."

"Good Morning,

Baggage Claims.

May I see your boarding pass?"

"Ah yes, I need to tell you that I will not be taking my baggage onboard with me today."

"OK ... so what would you like us to do with it?"

"I'm gonna' leave it right here at the airport."

"You mean ... right here on the floor? Are you abandoning your baggage?

"Absolutely! I don't want it anymore!"

"Very well. What's your flight number?"

"Freedom Flight 777 ..."

"OK, so your baggage will be dumped in the city trash by security, and you will not be charged for additional carry-on weight. Enjoy your flight."

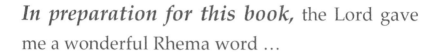

In preparation for this book, the Lord gave me a wonderful Rhema word ...

FLUSH

At first I thought ... flesh?

So I asked him, "Lord, what do you mean by flesh?" and he replied, "*Flush* ... not flesh."

That brought a smile to my face. So I began to study the word *flush* and this is what it means:

> *To get rid of ... to cleanse ... do away with ...*
> *... especially something bad.*

Suddenly, I had a new perspective on what the Lord was trying to say. Here it is ...

"I want my people to flush, get rid of, cleanse and do away with all those bad things of the past. I want them to release, let go, surrender and repent."

Matthew 24:22 declares, "And except those days be shortened, there should no flesh be saved, but for the elect's sake, those days shall be shortened."

Mark 11:25 also declares, "Whenever you stand praying, forgive, if you have anything against anyone, so that your Father who is in heaven will also forgive you your transgressions."

In the above verses we see two things: that toxic baggage in our souls, such as unforgiveness, hate and resentment, can escalate to the point of being classified by as sin by the Lord (although he is merciful to us); and that time is running out. Therefore, let us not be caught carrying resentment toward anyone.

We all have work to do, but we cannot do it carrying toxic poisons and bitterness around in our hearts, which can multiply and ruin *everything* in our lives! Sometimes the poisons are visible, sometimes invisible.

The word *invisible* means – *hidden, out of sight, unseen, concealed*. But more applicable to this subject, it means – *inward wounds and pain that is out of sight*. Invisible wounds can lie dormant for literally decades, deep within the inner belly, unseen with the natural eye, but very much alive on the inside, affecting everything we do and say and poison all our relationships. Next, let's explore the term *release*. This means *to let go, set free at liberty, be delivered from, unbind.* Apply this to the condition of the human heart and it means -- *to get rid of excess pain or hurt from the past.*

Men and women of God, we can no longer compromise his word! We can no longer stand at the baggage counter and reclaim ownership of our bad baggage, over and over! It's time to open up that baggage and throw the contents in the trash! In order to be released and set free, we must identify the pain and hurt in our flesh, and flush it out -- every negative thing in our hearts and minds!

What caused the pain? Was it abuse? What about abandonment or betrayal? Was it molestation, rejection, neglect? Physical or emotional abuse? Such events can cause severe symptoms of unforgiveness, bitterness, a broken heart, shattered self-esteem and all other kinds of emotional wounds. Most likely, there are several wounds that are dormant in you at this very moment that have spread to other areas of your life, perhaps even taken a toll on your health. Science proved long ago that:

1. Depression can manifest as actual, physical pain

2. Emotional trauma can paralyze its victims and/or make them suicidal

3. Stress causes diseases that can kill us!

Wouldn't now be a good time to flush out your heart and give yourself a brand new start? We represent the Lord! Romans 6:4(b) reminds us that, "As Christ is risen from the dead by the glory of the Father, we also may walk in NEWNESS OF LIFE."

Releasing and letting go is painful in the beginning of your healing process, but you must allow the Lord to remove it and get rid of all the ungodly spirits that may have you bound, simply by yielding to His Holy Spirit. Again, if pain and unforgiveness remain unchecked, the inward/invisible wounds can infect every area of our lives. Unforgiveness works like this:

> *You're planning to take a trip and fill one suitcase. Then you think of more things to stuff into that suitcase until it's over-loaded with excess baggage. What happens next is, we continue to add on, and add on, until we are completely overwhelmed with the excess!*

The human heart is no different than an over-stuffed suitcase. In the next few chapters we'll discuss the many kinds of excess baggage we experience in life and how to successfully flush them out.

On the next page is a brief synopsis as to how we'll do it ...

Interactive Chapter Instructions

1. Each chapter deals with a different kind of excess baggage.

2. An interactive journal has been included with this book. After you read each baggage chapter, open your journal and partake of the exercises. The journal will greatly assist you in the Flushing Process. Try it. It's fun!

3. After completing the Flushing Assignments in the journal, turn to the back of this book and read out loud *The Prayer of Acceptance & Deliverance*, after each chapter. If you're taking the class, we'll pray this together.

4. Then sign the contract with the Lord commemorating your Day of Deliverance.

The results will be wonderful!

Quick Tip …

Removing excess baggage from your soul may not be something you can do on your own.

The Flushing Process "gives permission" by your spoken word to the Lord to do this for you!

Luke 4.18 declares that the Lord is the one who opens prison doors and sets the captives free, not you!

It's all about you giving him *permission* to do so, not about you having to do it alone!

Let's begin …

Baggage 1

Unforgiveness

———⁓———

What excess, invisible baggage are you carrying? Is it something out of the past that is keeping you bound? Let's deal with unforgiveness first.

Unforgiveness is one of the hardest wounds to expel. The reason is -- the human body was not created to bear injustice, humiliation and indignation. Therefore, when we are attacked by these things, the God in us cries out for vindication! He is a God of vengeance and we have very own his nature. Our vengeance, however, can lead to murder and chaos, whereas his will be 100% righteous on Judgment Day. So let's leave vengeance to him!

Now, chances are that those who hurt us may never ask for forgiveness, therefore we have to expel the unforgiveness out of our souls, not necessarily because they deserve it, but FOR OUR OWN SURVIVAL!!

This invisible, excess baggage that keeps us bound in defeat can seriously hinder us from reaching the purpose, plan and destiny the Lord has ordained for our lives. It has to be FLUSHED OUT!

I can identify with unforgiveness. I was angry with my father when my mother passed away. My father seemed to be insensitive to my mother who was very ill and she eventually died a short time later. I took it so personally that I did not speak to my father for a very long time. On the day before Thanksgiving, I woke up and one of my knees was so swollen I could not walk. Fear came over me. I called my friend and he told me to go to the hospital.

When I arrived, the doctor ran tests on me from head to toe. He tried draining fluid from my knee but there was no fluid. However, my knee was three times its normal size. The hospital told me that they could not find any medical problems and advised me to elevate my leg. I was given a cane and crutches and sent home.

I had to crawl upstairs to my bedroom, was bedridden, unable to walk but a few steps and unable to prepare meals or be self-sufficient. The discomfort and swelling continued from Thanksgiving Day to the day before New Year's.

I had no pain, but the Spirit of the Lord spoke to me and said, "You must forgive your father." I rebelled in the beginning and tried to make excuses. I prayed, read my Bible and confessed all the healing scriptures over my knee, to no avail; but the Spirit of the Lord continued to speak to me. The healing of this invisible, inward wound would not expel until I acknowledged the spirit of unforgiveness controlling me.

This was the first invisible wound that I realized needed healing and deliverance. Furthermore, it reproduced itself into a "visible" condition on my physical body, and there were actually many more to follow.

As an entrepreneur, I owned a public relations company. One of my clients was interviewed on a television broadcast and my business telephone number was highlighted on the broadcast. One of the prayer-intercessors at the station telephoned my office and asked about my client participating in the Gospel concert they were producing. Aside from that business inquiry, the prayer intercessor also asked if I would like prayer for anything, and I said yes. The prayer was very powerful and that was when I realized the spirit of unforgiveness had become my excess baggage. It had attached itself to my internal wound. Right then and there I knew I needed deliverance and healing.

I telephoned my father and asked for his forgiveness. He never responded, but I was set free through my obedience! This was the day before New Year's and on New Year's Day my knee was *no longer swollen* but normal! It was a documented miracle seen by many people. I was healed and delivered instantly and celebrated Jesus the entire New Year's Day!

Once you begin to identify and acknowledge that you are carrying inward/invisible wounds you need to flush them out. Then, healing rushes in like cool, fresh water and washes all the poisons away. You'll feel lighter, fresher, happier!

Sometimes what you feel is a longer process, other times it happens instantly. Either way, it's imperative that you go deep into your inward belly and ask God to help you understand your motives and actions. Then ask him to help you release and let go of the torment that has held you in bondage for so long. Once you do, heaven breaks open and the Lord's blessings can once again flow freely into your life. We cannot undo what has been done, but we can change the future and never look back. Let go of your excess baggage!

Journal Exercise

Baggage 1 - Unforgiveness

In your journal, turn to Baggage 1 - Unforgiveness

Complete the written exercises.

Then turn to the back of the journal for:

The Prayer of Acceptance & Deliverance

Read this prayer with the rest of the class, or on your own, if not participating in the class.

As you read the prayer, please make a purposeful and earnest declaration to let go of Baggage 1, in the area of unforgiveness.

Baggage 2

Living In The Past

The excess baggage of living in the past and looking back on what once was (and is no more) can turn us into stone statues, just like Lot's wife. We can't move forward, upward, to the right or to the left. Walking backward makes us look abnormal and strange, and causes us to relive the hurt over and over.

For instance, I had a friend who refused to let go of the past situations in her life and all she wanted to talk about was her past, never looking forward to the future. I had moved on and outgrew her because we had nothing in more in common to talk about, nor any reason to continue a friendship. Some people like to remain STUCK in their past problems and *don't want to* move toward the future. Events that enslave us to the past can stem from abuse, abandonment, rejection and betrayal, all of which give rise to: anger, bitterness, unforgiveness, a broken heart, discouragement, resentment, jealousy, strife, contention, and other inward/invisible wounds.

As discussed in the prior chapter, such abnormalities cause severe pain and torment. Until you make the decision to release and let it go, you will be in bondage indefinitely. The Lord gives us a choice and whatever we decide, he will never go against our wills.

However, God's will is that you reach the purpose, plan and destiny that He has for your life. Jesus has guided and instructed me on how to use my own experience as a positive instead of negative way. Refusing to look back will bring forth additional healing that is needed.

Isaiah 53:5 states, "He was wounded for our transgressions and bruised for our iniquities. The chastisement of our peace was upon him and with his stripes we are healed."

We can only be healed through the blood of Jesus Christ. I am speaking of the invisible, unseen wounds that hold you in bondage and hinder your personal relationship with Jesus, who is our Chief Intercessor to the Father.

Romans 8:34 states, "Who then condemns us? No one; but Christ Jesus died for us, was raised to life for us and sits in the place of honor at God's right hand INTERCEDING for us."

Yes, we have Jesus, our High Priest, interceding on our behalf to the Father, in every situation seen or unseen, knowing or unknowing! In John 3:3, "Jesus answered and said unto him 'Except a man be born again, he cannot see the kingdom of God.'" Part of being born again means never walking in the oldness of life, but rather in the newness of life, flushing constantly that which paralyzes us.

Another invisible, spiritual wound is betrayal. Betrayal usually comes through someone close to you. Betrayal involves someone you trust being unfaithful, disloyal and deceptive toward you. For several years, I was in a place trying to hold onto someone who had made a choice to be with someone else. Yes, we were married but you cannot change anyone who's made a decision that they want to be with someone else. Due to my soul ties and commitment, I didn't want to let go and allow God to have his way in my life.

A soul tie is defined as a spiritual, emotional and/or physical connection to someone. I was independently fixated on keeping the relationship going, holding onto it and refusing to let go, but it was a marriage that was not working. It was a cycle of mental and emotional abuse but the Lord had other plans. My seventeen years of marriage and the soul tie caused my emotions to direct my path, instead of the Lord. I was unknowingly in bondage.

Sometimes, we become so dependent on *individuals* and *things* that we cannot see the forest for the trees. My husband, was the pastor of our church and God blessed us tremendously during the earlier years. We were successful entrepreneurs in real estate and operated several agencies for battered and abused women, children and families.

When you prolong a soul tie with an individual who no longer desires to be with you, you can become spiritually bound in your ministry as well, not just emotionally.

Journal Exercise

Baggage 2 – Living In The Past

In your journal, turn to Baggage 2 – Living In The Past

Complete the written exercises.

Then turn to the back of the journal for:

> *The Prayer of Acceptance & Deliverance*

Read this prayer with the rest of the class, or on your own, if not participating in the class.

As you read the prayer, please make a purposeful and earnest declaration to let go of Baggage 2, in the area of living in the past.

Baggage 3

Guilt

———————～———————

Although, I had been praying, fasting and reading the Word, nothing changed the relationship between me and my husband. Later, I learned that I was praying the wrong way. One day the Spirit of the Lord spoke to me and said, "Your prayer should be about *you*. I desire *your* purpose, plan and destiny, because *your* husband belongs to me."

The Lord wanted me to release and let go. The scriptures teach that the husband and wife have authority over one another, therefore, I'm sure that psychologically I still felt that I had a right and an obligation to keep our marriage together. But what if the husband or wife does not want to return? If not, we are no longer spiritually or eternally responsible for their behavior. During this time, the Spirit of the Lord spoke to me again and said, "Your prayer should be about my purpose, plan and destiny for your life," in other words, not my husband's. My former husband was from then on the Lord's responsibility.

I love the Lord. However, I was not trusting God who is my Comforter, Healer and Deliverer. As discussed earlier, carrying inward/invisible wounds can cause you to manifest sickness, disease, and psychological problems. I began to have high blood pressure, anxiety, depression and had to go to a chiropractor to align my body. One day the doctor said, "You can change your situation and condition but it's your choice. Whatever you're going through, you need to get rid of it. Let it go! It's weighing you down both physically and mentally."

After this, Satan's attacks against our marriage became more forceful, utilizing my husband with more demonic behaviors than before, by inflicting more pain, abuse and anguish. He spent days away from home. Days became weeks and weeks became months. He spent money by the thousands, failed to show up for church and abandoned his call to the ministry. One day my husband wrote our church a letter stating that he was taking a sabbatical and that I would be taking over as pastor. This caused severe pain to the entire congregation and myself. As a result, I took in the entire impact of guilt associated with this fall-out. As the pastor's wife, I felt I had a responsibility to feed God's sheep. My accountability was to God for those souls. My husband was caught up in a snare. I don't want to appear that I am judging or criticizing him, but my former husband allowed Satan to come in to steal, kill and destroy. Take a look:

John 10:10

Satan comes only to steal, kill and destroy,
but I have to come to give you life, and that
more abundantly.

Soon, we had no communication at all. Do you continue to blame yourself for someone else's behavior? Do you convict and persecute yourself because a relationship collapsed with a spouse, child, relative or employer? Perhaps you've done something that you just can't forgive yourself for. We begin focusing on what we could have done, should not have done, and how our lives might have been different. Guilt can beat up our minds, but we have the option of just releasing and letting it go.

After that Jesus became my husband. In fact, he was my friend, protector and everything I had. The more I prayed the more comfort came upon me. I just wanted to be in his presence at all times. A peace I had never felt before flooded over me. During those times, the Spirit would speak to me saying, "Pray without ceasing for him." The more I prayed, the more I felt the comfort of Jesus as he released my excess baggage.

My thoughts began to turn toward the goodness of Jesus then, and how much he loved me. Before long, I felt the excess baggage dissipate as his healing and deliverance completely engulfed my soul.

The more hurts you surrender to the Lord, the stronger his healing power becomes. The Word of God became my best tool. It gave me peace in time of loneliness and showed me how to release all things that were not of His Word. Release, let go and cast all your cares on God for He will give you rest! Jesus made me to understand that he is all knowing, all seeing and all-powerful. Sometimes our emotions cause us to feel that we are in love, but our minds can bring confusion to our emotions. Sometimes we continue to go in and out of relationships with the same negative person, when the Lord has already set us free and released us to move forward. But this cycle brings only more pain, resentment, anger, hatred, bitterness and unforgiveness.

Love is not an emotion. It's an unconditional, spiritual connection that God provides for mankind. It's a commitment of sacrificial action toward another person. Many times people are unable to release their inward feelings because they don't want to hurt someone or lose that relationship and/or friendship. Not letting go of someone because you don't want to hurt them, is *the cousin* of the guilt baggage. Relationships should never be fostered through guilt. Never feel guilt from your past. Never look back in the rear view mirror. Instead, look forward!

Journal Exercise

Baggage 3 – Guilt

In your journal, turn to Baggage 3 – Guilt.

Complete the written exercises.

Then turn to the back of the journal for:

The Prayer of Acceptance & Deliverance

Read this prayer with the rest of the class, or on your own, if not participating in the class.

As you read the prayer, please a make purposeful and earnest declaration to let go of Baggage 3, in the area of guilt.

Baggage 4

Self-Loathing

As discussed in the prior chapter, during this time, the Spirit of the Lord spoke to me and said, "Your prayer should be about my purpose, plan and destiny for your life."

I was in a place of having lost my identity. I was so broken that the reality of who I was no longer had any meaning. By suppressing my real feelings, emotions, hurts, and pains, I became an enabler to someone else's fallen lifestyle, thereby not fulfilling my own dreams and purpose.

Although the Lord had given me signs before these things happened, I chose to ignore them and wouldn't let go. My mind was closed to reality because my entire identity was wrapped up in this marriage. My fear was that I did not want to be alone. You must realize that you have to *LOVE YOU* before anyone else and trust in God's Word that He is your burden-barer.

But self-loathing, also known as 'shattered self-esteem,' never allows us to love our own person. Unbeknownst to many, the Lord does give us permission to love ourselves first. Here's why -- If we cannot love and take care of ourselves first, we cannot love and take care of others! Thus, we are useless to the kingdom of God. Take a look:

Mark 12:31

Thou shalt love the Lord thy God with all thy heart, soul, mind and strength. This is the first commandment. The **second is this: Thou shalt love thy neighbor as thyself. There is **none other** commandment **greater** than these.

Notice the astounding points in the **second commandment. 1) The love we have for our neighbors should be just as strong as the love we have for our own person, and ... 2) This JUST AS CRUCIAL as loving God!

As I was releasing and letting go of my excess baggage, I had to love me *first* before I could be delivered and healed. I had to flush out the self-loathing baggage. Because of my failed marriage, the 'I'm Not Worthy' tapes spun round and round in my head until I was convinced that I was nothing, which mutated into my shattered self-esteem.

The Lord had to purge and flush out this darkness so that I could move on with my own purpose, plan and destiny. He had to destroy the 'I'm Not Worthy' tapes in my head, and reconstruct my self-image until I once again understood that I am *His Royal Diadem!*

At first, I didn't know how to trust God enough to believe that he would heal me and set me free. This is a normal human condition. Job of the Old Testament held the same viewpoint of God. Take a look –

Job 9:16
"If I had called, and he had answered me,
I still would not believe that he would
answer my voice!"

Job suffered of a shattered self-esteem. Notice that he said, even if God was standing in front of his face, he still would not believe that God would want to help him. With all the favor that God loaded on him as the wealthiest and most favored man in all the region, he still had no inclination as to his royal identity. With such lack of faith no wonder God could not do a thing to help him before the destruction hit.

If we refuse to believe that God will help us, let alone love us, then many times God cannot move on our be-half. We have to *trust in him* that he will help us.

Self-loathing is a baggage we have to release and let go of immediately. You must learn to focus your mind on what the Lord says about you! Focus your mind on your self-worth. What does the Word say about? To achieve this and benefit from it, you have to meditate on His Word daily, stay motivated and remain focused on who you are in him. It's time to put new tape record-ings in your head.

On the next page is an exact outline as to how
the Lord sees you through his own eyes.

Repeat these confessions with me daily:

- I am the ambassador for Christ (2 Cor 5:20).

- I am the chosen generation, a royal priesthood, a holy nation (1 Pet 2:9).

- I am the righteousness of God in Jesus Christ (2 Cor 5:21).

- I am the head and not the tail, above only and never beneath (Deut 28:13).

- I am the light of the world (Matt 5:14).

- For God has not given me a spirit of fear, but of power, love, and a sound mind (2 Tim 1:7).

- I am forgiven of all my sins and washed in the Blood (Eph 1:7).

- I am a joint-heir with Christ (Rom 8:17).

- I am holy and without blame before Him in love (Ephesians 1:4; 1 Pet 1:16).

- I have the mind of Christ (1 Cor 2:16; Phil 2:5).

- I can do all things in Christ (Phil 4.13).

Ask the Lord to give you not only natural strength but also supernatural strength to overcome the negative images you have of yourself. Ask him to show you how you look TO HIM. He will lift the heavy burdens from your heart, body and mind and make everything new!

Flush out all that darkness, release it and let go! Remember no more your afflictions, obsessions and misery. When we have hope in our Lord Jesus he will break off the chains of bondage from your being and give you a NEW self-image, reflecting his power and his love!

Journal Exercise

Baggage 4 – Self-Loathing

In your journal, turn to Baggage 4 – Self-Loathing

Complete the written exercises.

Then turn to the back of the journal for:

> *The Prayer of Acceptance & Deliverance*

Read this prayer with the rest of the class, or on your own, if not participating in the class.

As you read the prayer, please make a purposeful and earnest declaration to let go of Baggage 4, in the area of self-loathing.

Baggage 5

Anger & Rage

———————～———————

Anger is a normal motion of human nature. We were created in the likeness of God with the full range of his own emotions!

Anger is not always a bad thing! We become angry when we see children mistreated at the hands of negligent parents. We become angry when someone destroys our property, so on and so forth.

Jesus got angry one day too. He walked into the temple of Jerusalem, looked around and saw all the merchants setting up shop in his Father's house, as though it were an outdoor flea market. So he found some leather cords, braided them into a strap and then whipped that place to shreds!

We experience anger and righteous indignation about a wide variety of wrongs in the world. That's when anger rises up and says, "Enough is enough!"

Anger, in the healthy sense, protects us and provides us with the moral compass to distinguish between right and wrong. We have the right to righteous indignation. Take a look:

Ephesians 4:26

Be angry but do not sin. Do not let the sun go down on your wrath …

Matthew 18:15-17

If anyone sins against you, go and tell them their fault in private. If they hear you, you have gained your brother …

These instructions tell us it's OK to be angry. Do speak out your anger and do get it off your chest quickly, preferably before the sun goes down! But if the offender will not hear you, at one point or another we will have to let it go and flush it. The reason is, anger can be a toxic poison if left unattended! This is why the Word said to flush it out before the sun goes down.

Righteous anger is a good thing, but when abused comes with serious consequences. Take for instance Miriam, the elder sister of Moses and Aaron. Miriam and Aaron started a grumbling campaign against Moses because he had married a Cushite woman. However, the Lord never had a problem with Moses' Cushite wife, so what right did they have to speak against her? The incident, recorded in Numbers Chapter 12, resulted with the Lord striking Miriam with leprosy. Had Aaron not begged for her life, she would have died that way. The Lord healed Miriam seven days later, but this remains a crucial lesson for us to manage anger righteously, and more importantly, to quickly move forward from there -- back into the fresh air of forgiveness.

Out of control rage is not a good thing. Rage is an out of control emotion that can get us into serious trouble. Rage kills and maims people, and the effects are irreversible.

It's extremely important to turn the inner/invisible inner wound of anger over to the Lord during these exercises and flush it out before it escalates to rage.

Do you have anger toward a family member, spouse, friend, co-worker, church or something that triggers your rage? Before your rage causes the loss of some-one's life, limb or property, think it through carefully. Remember that you could spend the rest of your life constrained, only to lose your children, home, career, ministry, and good name in the community. Therefore, expel this poisonous, excess baggage and flush it out of your system!

Rage is fueled by unforgivness and/or jealousy. It's something you don't need right now in your life! You have a new destiny to fulfill, new people to meet, new places to go and precious talents to use! Right?

Journal Exercise

Baggage 5 – Anger & Rage

In your journal, turn to Baggage 5 – Anger & Rage

Complete the written exercises.

Then turn to the back of the journal for:

The Prayer of Acceptance & Deliverance

Read this prayer with the rest of the class, or on your own, if not participating in the class.

As you read the prayer, please make a purposeful and earnest declaration to let go of Baggage 5, in the area of anger and rage.

It's time to

Flush in a

New Awakening!

Luke 4.18

"The Spirit of the Lord is upon me because he has anointed me to preach the Gospel to the poor. He has sent me to heal the broken-hearted, to preach deliverance to the captives, and recovering of sight to the blind, to set at liberty them that are bruised."

Flush In A New
Spiritual Awakening

Our Lord's mercy and compassion will not fail because his love, gentleness and faithfulness are new every morning. As you flush out all uncleanliness, release and let go, the Lord will give you a new, spiritual awakening. Hope and peace will bring you unspeakable joy. Doors of blessings will burst open that you never imagined possible. You'll experience a crisp, new focus as to who you are and where you are going. When you let go of your baggage, the Lord will perform a complete 180-degree turn-around in your life. In fact, turning lives around is his specialty.

As you flush out the excess baggage, God will also deliver you from tormenting, demonic spirits that have kept you in bondage. Take a look --

Luke 4.18

The Spirit of the Lord is upon me, because
he has anointed me to proclaim good news
to the poor. He has sent me to proclaim freedom for the prisoners and recovery of sight
for the blind, to set the oppressed free.

Jesus, the Anointed of the Lord, wants to deliver every
area of our lives. Ruth and Naomi were two examples
in the Old Testament who were able to release excess
baggage very quickly and move forward. After losing
her husband and two sons, Naomi decided to return to
her home of Judah. Naomi had two daughters-in-law
with her. She encouraged them to return to their own
families in Moab, and while Oprah returned home,
Ruth cleaved unto Naomi and said, "Don't urge me to
leave you or turn back from you. Where you go I will
go, and where you stay I will stay. Your people will be
my people and your God my God ..." Ruth 1:16-18

Naomi and Ruth were determined to release and let
go of their past. They moved on and trusted God. The
result was, Ruth was remarried to the wealthiest and
most influential man in Judah and actually became the

lineage of Christ Jesus because of her marriage to Boaz. When we let go of excess baggage the Lord can once again reignite the royal plan meant for each of us, individually.

In the Old Testament we also see the account of Queen Esther, the beautiful woman who was married to the Persian King Ahasuerus, also known as Xerxes II. During the Hebrews' 70-year captivity in Babylon, from 607-537 BC, an evil palace-insider named Haman, hated the Hebrews, turned the king against them and tried to have them all killed—and it almost worked. The king signed the death decree and the genocide was officially scheduled that following week. But unbeknownst to the king and Haman, Esther was also a Hebrew.

When Esther's cousin, Mordecai, told her about the plot she didn't lose her focus and immediately began to fast, pray and seek wisdom from God on how to stop the upcoming genocide of her people.

Queen Esther was a woman of high integrity and respect. She remained focused on what God needed her to do for his people and wouldn't allow any interference in her assignment. She trusted God for the removal of Haram, the current excess baggage in her life, and God certainly did remove it. For having plotted to kill the queen, King Ahasuerus hanged Haram on the very gallows he had built for the Jews.

Now, the point of this story is this: Unlike the doubting Job, who refused to believe that God would ever help him, Esther immediately ran to the Lord! And if the Lord removed Esther's baggage in the form of a genocidal murderer, it is NOTHING for him to supernaturally remove your inner wounds as well.

All you have to do is schedule the appointment!

During the flushing process, our focus is to be in God's presence, to receive and obey his instructions. The prayers of the righteous avail much. Esther, with the help of the Lord, preserved the Hebrew family line. What will you save once you finally expel your excess baggage?

The Flush!

I am now speaking to saved persons who have experi-enced trauma and abuse at the hands of other people, preferably, those who have accepted Jesus Christ as their Lord and Savior, with the evidence of a personal relationship with him.

As discussed earlier, chances are those who hurt you may never come forward and apologize. Therefore, it's imperative for your own preservation and survival that you flush out the darkness, uncleanliness, corruption and filthiness that was no doubt planted in you by something or someone that hurt you. The Lord has to be in complete control during the flushing process of expelling the excess baggage. Let's take a look why ...

Dr. Patricia Logan-Miles

Reasons to Let Go and Move On

1. Someone's negativity is rubbing off on you. Do not allow their negative karma to cause you to become cynical or negative

2. You have outgrown certain negative individuals in your social circle, with whom you no longer share the same interests, as evidenced by constant clashes

3. The individual makes you unhappy and, more often than not, their personality irritates you

4. You've developed health problems

5. You've lost jobs, income and friends

6. You suffer of insomnia and problems getting up in the morning

7. The spirit of fear has you bound

8. You have problems releasing the past. Wounds of the past are keeping you in bondage

9. Situations of the past are cluttering your mind and keeping you from fulfilling your future

10. You are holding unhealthy grudges, for instance: resentment, anger, jealousy, bitterness and unforgiveness, which keep you from reaching your God-given destiny

11. You are stuck in every area of life and do not seem to be moving forward. You feel as though you are dying slowly and that there is nothing left for you in life

Sometimes we have to seek spiritual counseling if our situations are overwhelming. Chances are, you may not be able to flush your baggage alone and you'll need support.

In either case, the above symptoms are enough motivation for any one of us to flush the excess baggage and fight for a new start! Flushing these things is a step of elevation toward your higher destiny, where all the desires of your heart await you. The victory is yours for the taking!

You are about to look through a window directly into your future, once you've flushed your baggage. It's enough to get you seriously excited to start afresh!

The promises on the next page are from God's word. If you're carrying around toxic baggage, the blessings can be seriously blocked, because harboring them is a form of unforgiveness, and worse … "anti-faith."

Remember Esther and Job? One believed immediately that God would help, while the other never even called on his name! The following blessings were cut with the blood of useless animals under the Old Blood Covenant. Just think of how much MORE we are entitled to under the New Covenant cut with the pristine Blood of Christ!

What You Get …

Once You Get Flushed!

You are about to look through a window directly into your future, once you've flushed your baggage. It's enough to get you seriously excited to start afresh!

The promises on the next page are from God's word. If you're carrying around toxic baggage, the blessings can be seriously blocked, because harboring them is a form of unforgiveness, and worse … "anti-faith."

Remember Esther and Job? One believed immediately that God would help, while the other never even called on his name!

The following blessings were cut with the blood of useless animals under the Old Blood Covenant. Just think how much MORE we are entitled to, under the New Blood Covenant cut with the pristine Blood of Christ!

Deuteronomy 28:1-14

You will be blessed ...

- In the city and in the country (**Career, promotions and favor!)

- In the fruit of your body (**marriage and children!)

- In your crops and livestock (**food and supplies!)

- In your going in and going out (**general wellbeing!)

- Your enemies will flee from you in seven different directions (**divine protection!)

- In your storehouses (**immunity from recession!)

- And all you put your hand to will prosper (**success in business and ministry!)

- In your land (**property ownership!)

- You will lend and never borrow (**debt cancellation!)

- You'll be above and never beneath (**a respected pillar of society!)

You'll Also Receive A
Double-Portion Call to Ministry!

Once you flush your baggage, the Lord will fire you up for ministry and/or your career path as never before!

Proverbs 16:18

"Your gifts will bring you before presidents, government officials and the world-wide, evangelical theater."

Matthew 28:18-20

"All authority in heaven and on Earth will be given to you! Go and make disciples of all nations …"

1 Corinthians 12:8-10

"For to one is given the word of wisdom through the Spirit, to another the word of knowledge … to another the gift faith … gifts of healing … miracles … prophecy … discerning of spirits … diverse tongues and interpretation of tongues."

OK, so here's the question ...

Considering the outrageous blessings

Designed just for you ...

Do you really want to

Keep nursing your old, tired wounds?

Flush them out!

Enter Your New Life !!

The God Plan

We all have choices. We can make negative or positive decisions. We as humans are creatures of habit. Habits can become addictive in a positive or negative way, but it is your choice. The unfortunate situations in our lives, through no fault of our own, caused us to feel that this is the only life we will ever have, and we must therefore accept it. We all have challenges in our lives but we must continue to seek the purpose, plan and destiny that God created for us. We were not created to be failures. As creatures of habit we like being in control, whether for good or evil. Your thoughts can cause your focus to become distracted and lead you into a path of destruction. Living on Earth, the enemy many times tries to set strongholds, obstacles and temptations before us. We should always remain focused in the right direction. Bad habits, once they gain control of your mind and body, can make releasing and letting go very difficult. Bad habits that you hold onto such as, smoking, alcohol, drugs, lust, pornography, overeating, the occult and sensual activities are psychological and physical strongholds that are of the flesh, brought on by the bad choices we make and can cause you to lose everything -- your job, family, marriage, home and so forth. If your deliverance from inward/invisible wounds does not manifest almost immediately, seek spiritual counseling and a reputable rehabilitation center to help you. The Lord honors prayer and medicine and will use both to get you well.

Many times we give individuals the opportunity to influence our lives, believing they have our best interests at heart, when in fact, they display negative motives and behaviors that are contrary to our health and freedom. The root cause of all inward/invisible wounds can always be traced to issues of low self-esteem, abuse, abandonment, discouragement, loneliness, despair and rejection; and co-dependent individuals will use those inward/invisible wounds to keep you bound to them. As you set objectives and goals, time management is very important throughout the flushing process. For instance, if you want to be delivered from anger, your anger needs to be clearly defined (preferably on paper if you are not participating the class exercises.)

Write out your complaints against the events and/or individuals that caused your wounds. As you write out your grievances, do so with the expectation that you will also schedule a date to release and let go of this toxic baggage, once and for all.

Moving forward requires a GOD HABIT. I encourage you to make a list of objectives and goals that you want for your life – things that make you excited to get up in the morning! Write a NEW GOD PLAN in your journal. Identify your objective as to when, where and how you want it accomplished. Here are some organizational points to help you get started:

The New God Plan

1. Objective: Write down your objective.

2. Plan: What do you plan to accomplish?

3. Purpose: What is your idea or intention?

4. Destiny: Write down your vision.

5. Future: Where do you see yourself in 5 years?

The New God Habit

1. Accept the truth and be thankful.

2. Write down what your invisible and inward wounds are and begin to release them one by one to the Lord.

3. Distance yourself from all negative influences, such as questionable people, events, television programs and derogatory music, etc., that will keep you bound to the baggage.

4. Move on, move forward, move on up! Focus and see yourself and the things around you with a new set of eyes – as royalty – the way the Lord sees you!

5. Seek the Lord for his wisdom, understanding and knowledge. Proverbs: 3:5-6 instructs us to, "Trust in the Lord with all your heart and lean not to your own understanding. In all your ways, acknowledge him and he shall direct your paths."

6. Change your focus only on what you *can change* about yourself at the start.

7. Take note of things you cannot change for now. Do not waste your time on things you can't do anything about.

8. Claim ownership and full control of your life. Take authority over your life, desires and goals. No one is in control of your life but YOU when submitted to the Lord!

9. Take a chance! When life sets up a challenge there is always a reason in Christ. Nothing ever happens by chance in Christ. During the challenge, God will teach, direct, and guide you into your destiny.

Holding onto inner/invisible wounds is painful, but you can release them and let go. Remember, Jesus is in control and he will come through as promised, but we must stand, have faith, and trust in Him only. Trouble lasts only as long as we allow it, but if we hand it over to the Lord, he will carry you all the way through. He is the burden-carrier! Make him your New God Plan.

Isaiah 43.26

Put me in remembrance; let us plead together: set forth thy cause, that thou mayest be justified.

Release & Let Go of

Excess Baggage!

————————⁓————————

This book was written to teach us how to survive after releasing your excess baggage. You can survive after your soul has been torn to shreds! You may have suffered as the victim of brokenness, hurt, pain and shame or some other unknown circumstances; only you and God knows what happened. But God can hear you and will help you when you come to him.

In times past many of us suffered needlessly under the hands of cruel or unjust people. We are all victims of something or someone but God brought us through it all. Nevertheless, many people are still angry at God. They believe his hand was involved in the horrific abuses committed against them, or that he sat by watching on without doing one thing about it. But here is what we need to remember: Evil caused those things to happen to you not God! When evil is mixed with free will, it's the most destructive thing in all the universe. Therefore, it is absolutely crucial to your very survival that you understand WHO did those things to you, and who DID NOT. Take a look –

John 10:10

[Satan] comes only to steal, kill and destroy, but I have to come to give you life, and that more abundantly.

James 1:16-17

Do not be deceived, my beloved brethren. Every good gift and every perfect gift is from above, and comes down from the Father of lights, with whom there is no variation or shadow of turning.

James 1:13

If any man is **tested**, let him NOT SAY I am **tested** of God, for God cannot be **tested,** nor does he **test ANYONE.**

Strong's Concordance, Greek Word "TEST" # 3985 & 3986

God is the source of all light, physically, intellectually and spiritually and he does not change. Notice that --

John 10:10 tells us exactly WHO the destroyer is and it's Satan, the devil -- *never* God.

James 1:16-17 declares that God is NEVER involved in evil, and that his character will never change on this.

James 1:13 confirms that he never tests us with heart-break and disasters -- and why would he? To make life even more difficult than it already is?

Next, we need to understand that the Lord will give you JUSTICE, in this life or the next. If wrongdoers confess their sins before they die, their eternal destiny is between them and God alone. But if not, rest assured, God will hand out justice. By now, you should feel 50% lighter knowing the Lord had nothing to do with your heartbreak. This book is designed to help you with the other 50% -- which now brings us back to the main point. Your relationship with the Lord is the most important in your entire life. He understands everything and is standing by, ready to hear your heart. And guess what! He will JUSTIFY YOU. This promise is worth another look:

Isaiah 43.26
Put me in remembrance; let us plead together: set forth thy cause, that thou mayest be justified.

That's right – bring your grievance to him! Release and let go of the excess baggage in your heart! Be healed and let God's justification wash you clean! Once you go through the process, here are the Lord's thoughts toward you:

Jeremiah 29:11-13
For I know the thoughts that I think toward you, saith Jehovah, thoughts of peace, and not of evil, to give you a future and a hope! And ye shall call upon me, and ye shall go and pray unto me, and I will hear you. And ye shall seek me, and find me, when ye shall search for me with all your heart.

As discussed earlier, when you set objectives and goals, time management is important for each healing session. If you are going through the Flushing Process on your own, outside the class, be sure to do the following:

On the Day of the Flushing Appointment

1. Make sure your notes on each baggage are clearly defined. State the reasons for your wounds.

2. Then mark your calendar and make the appointment with the Lord.

3. Turn off the TV and your cell phone

4. Close the curtains

5. Eat and drink ahead of time

6. Have *The Prayer of Acceptance and Deliverance* ready.

7. And get to a place where you can pray out loud.

During your conversations with the Lord, speak the words burning in your inner belly that you need to release. Be reconciled to your Father in heaven. He stands ready to enter deliberations with you. And after that…

THE VICTORY IS YOURS!

The
Prayer of
Acceptance & Deliverance

The Prayer of
Acceptance & Deliverance

On the next page is the prayer that we will be praying together and come into agreement. It's call *The Prayer of Acceptance and Deliverance* and was given to me by the Lord, especially with you and me in mind.

The prayer will help you to accept, release and let go of those inward/invisible wounds. You are now on your way to total healing and being set free from the bondage of excess baggage.

Let's pray together …

Thank You Father …

In the Name of Jesus …

For the gift of your son Jesus. Thank you also for bending your ear low and listening to me. Father, I make these confessions by the words of my mouth, knowing that you will honor my faith, and that you will bring these things to pass. I now confess these things to you:

Father, in the name of Jesus, I refuse to fear any longer. I have no fear because there is no fear in God.

I am not a failure and I am not afraid of what people can do to me. I have faith and trust in you, Lord, to bring me into the purpose, plan, and destiny that you have designed for me. The end has not come yet!

Greater is He who is in me, to cause me to succeed, than he who is in the world, who wants to me to fail.

I am a world overcomer! My faith is the victory that overcomes the world!

I can do all things through Christ who strengthens me. I have the victory and Jesus is His Name. I have it now. I can see it through the eyes of my faith.

Amen … SO BE IT!

1st John 4:18 says, "There is no fear in love. Perfect love casts out fear… "

The more I release and let go of my pain and broken heart, the more healing and deliverance comes over me.

By casting all my cares and burdens upon you, Lord, you will protect, heal, and deliver me from all my problems.

Lord, you know all the hurts and wounds that I suffered and the many times I have been rejected. You know the things that have been dormant in my inner belly.

Father, by a deliberate act of my will, I lay down and give up all bitterness, resentment, hatred, rejection, abandonment, abuse, my broken heart, unforgiveness and the rebellion that came from those wounds!

I release and let them go now from this day forth, in the Name of Jesus.

(Now read the names of all those who wounded you. Read from your sheet of paper)

I now release myself in forgiveness toward all those who have trespassed against me and wounded me in any way. Help me to do it, Lord! I release the excess baggage that I have held onto. I now let it go and will no longer remember the past.

I now come to you as my Deliverer. Your Word promises in Joel and Romans that whoever calls upon your name shall be delivered. In your name, Jesus, I ask you to deliver me and set me free from all inward/invisible wounds.

Lord, I release myself from all the power of demonic spirits and I will now walk and live in the full forgiveness of everyone that has ever wounded or rejected me in any way or at any time.

I thank you Lord for setting me free!

I resist and renounce the spirit of rejection, abuse, abandonment, resentment, despair, fear and other sources, and I command them to leave NOW!

I renounce the spirit of inward/invisible and spiritual wounds, and I command them to leave NOW!

Thank you, Father, for the work you have done in me.

My healing will bring great glory to your name and deliverance to many others.

In Jesus' name I pray. Amen.

Closing Words ...

———~———

The Word of God became my best tool. It gave me peace in my darkest hour. The Lord showed me how to release all negative things in my life. Jesus made me to understand that He is all knowing, all seeing, and all powerful. His Holy Spirit dwells within us. The prayer you just read was inspired by the Lord Jesus Christ to set you free from the bondage of excess baggage. You must understand that there will be a process of time for you to receive your total healing and deliverance, because you have been carrying this excess baggage for a while. But I am grateful to the Lord and those who prayed for me during my time of great need, as I will do with you. And like their prayers, I trust this book will be of great comfort to you as well. He will keep you.

Dr. Patricia Logan-Miles

Special Thanks to ...

Evangelist Leon Isaac Kennedy
Kennedy Healing Love Ministries
Producer, Writer, Actor
Burbank, California

Mr. Marvin Miller
Founder, President
20/20 Goodyear Media Solutions
Moreno Valley, California

Dr. Vicki Lee
Founder, CEO
Saints of Value World Ministries
Downey, California

And all my friends and prayer partners ...

Thank you!

Contact Information

We hope you enjoyed Dr. Patricia Logan-Miles' critical examination of managing inner healing.

To order additional books, go to:

www.HavenofComfort.com

Or write:
Haven of Comfort Ministries
3129 Hacienda Blvd., #365
Hacienda Heights, CA 91745

To schedule a speaking engagement, write:

Email: drpatmiles@yahoo.com

Dr. Logan-Miles' books are also on Amazon:

Search for ... Patricia Logan Miles

Made in the USA
Middletown, DE
27 September 2021